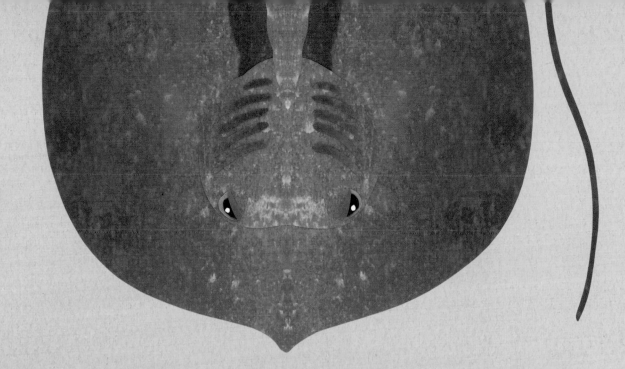

APEX PREDATORS

The World's Deadliest Hunters, Past and Present

Steve Jenkins

Houghton Mifflin Harcourt   Boston   New York

Predators are animals that kill and eat other animals. The first predator lived in the sea about 600 million years ago. It was probably some sort of worm, and it hunted other slow-moving, soft-bodied sea-floor creatures. Millions of years passed, and prey animals evolved new and better ways of not getting eaten. Some grew hard shells or armored skin. Others got larger, faster, or more difficult to spot. To survive, predators had to keep up. Their bodies got stronger and their senses grew keener. Their weapons—teeth, claws, beaks, and poison—became deadlier.

Many predators risk becoming prey themselves, the victims of bigger or stronger animals. But in every habitat, past and present, there have been a few apex predators—creatures too tough, too big, or too well-armed to be hunted by other animals. This book is about these killers—the apex predators of their time and place.

The **terror bird** stalked the plains of South America 15 million years ago. This killer stood ten feet (3 meters) tall, and it could run as fast as a horse.

Top predators of today...

The **Siberian tiger** is an apex predator of the Asian forests. It is so big and strong that no other animal dares attack it.

The Siberian tiger stalks a deer, water buffalo, or other large grazing animal. With a sudden charge, it knocks its victim to the ground and kills it with a bite to the throat.

8 FEET
(2½ METERS)

...and yesterday.

Many of the most terrifying animal killers pursued their prey thousands or millions of years ago. *Tyrannosaurus rex,* one of the top predators of all time, died out 66 million years ago.

40 FEET
(12 METERS)

This fierce dinosaur could bite off 500 pounds (227 kilograms) of flesh with one snap of its jaws.

Island monster

The **Komodo dragon** is the world's largest lizard. Sometimes it is a scavenger, feeding on dead animals. At other times it is a deadly predator, lying in wait, then leaping on a deer, goat, or water buffalo. It will kill and eat other Komodo dragons, and it occasionally attacks humans.

Many of today's apex predators, such as the Komodo dragon and the great white shark, are familiar. Other modern-day killers are less well known because they are rare or live in remote parts of the world.

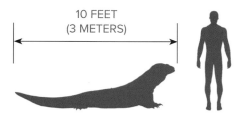

10 FEET
(3 METERS)

These huge reptiles live on a few islands in the southwest Pacific Ocean. They have razor-sharp teeth, powerful claws, and venomous saliva.

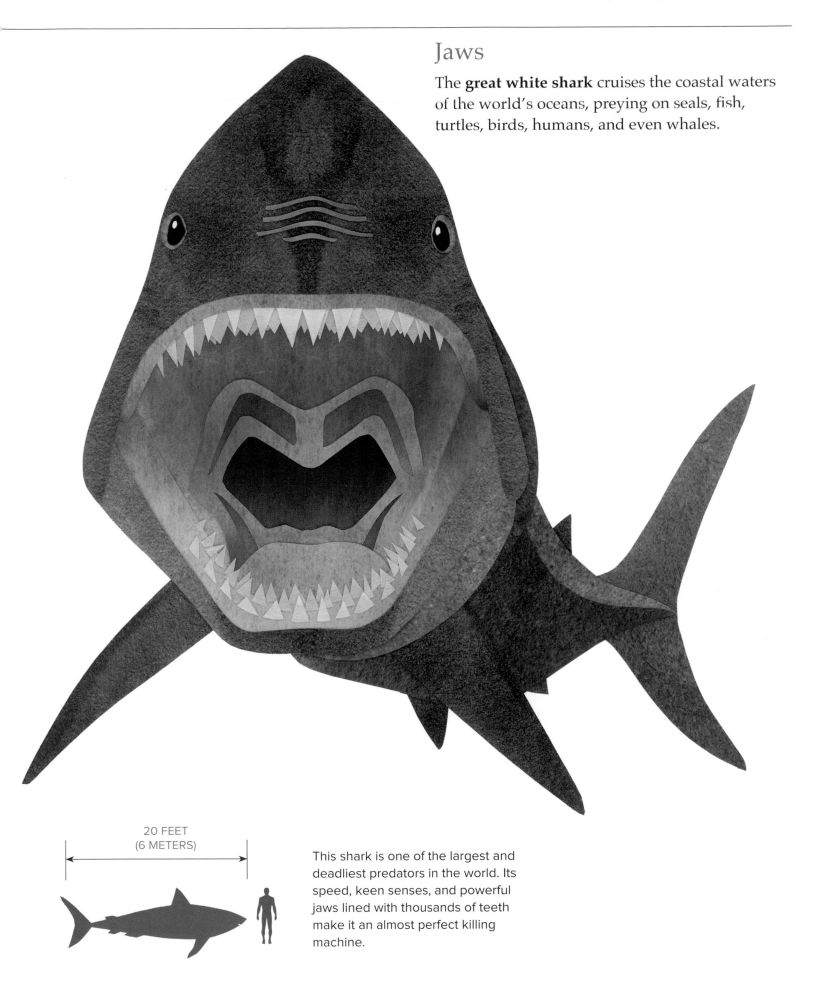

Jaws

The **great white shark** cruises the coastal waters of the world's oceans, preying on seals, fish, turtles, birds, humans, and even whales.

20 FEET
(6 METERS)

This shark is one of the largest and deadliest predators in the world. Its speed, keen senses, and powerful jaws lined with thousands of teeth make it an almost perfect killing machine.

Strength in numbers

Hunting in packs of as many as thirty animals, **African wild dogs** patiently pursue an antelope, wildebeest, or zebra until their prey drops from exhaustion.

39 INCHES
(1 METER)

These dogs share their habitat with bigger and stronger hunters, including lions and leopards. Nevertheless, they are some of the most successful predators on earth, with nine out of ten hunts ending in a kill.

Shockingly effective

The **electric eel** lurks in the rivers and streams of tropical South America. It zaps fish, amphibians, and other small animals with a powerful electric charge, then gulps them down while they are stunned and helpless.

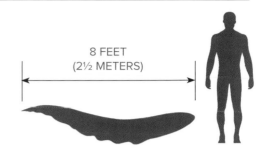

8 FEET
(2½ METERS)

This fish also uses electricity to defend itself. Any animal that attacks it risks getting jolted by a shock strong enough to stun a horse or kill a human.

Agile hunter

The **fossa** (*fos-uh*) is found only on the island of Madagascar. It is an excellent climber, and it stalks its prey—lemurs, wild pigs, birds, reptiles, and small mammals—in the treetops and on the ground.

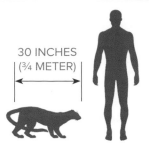

30 INCHES
(¾ METER)

The fossa looks like a cat, but it is more closely related to a mongoose.

Mind the barb!

The **giant freshwater ray** is one of the world's largest freshwater fish. It sucks clams and crayfish from the muddy river bottoms of Southeast Asia, where it earns its apex status by being the biggest predator in its habitat.

This ray locates its prey by detecting the faint electric field that all living creatures produce. At the base of its tail is a sharp, venomous barb used for defense.

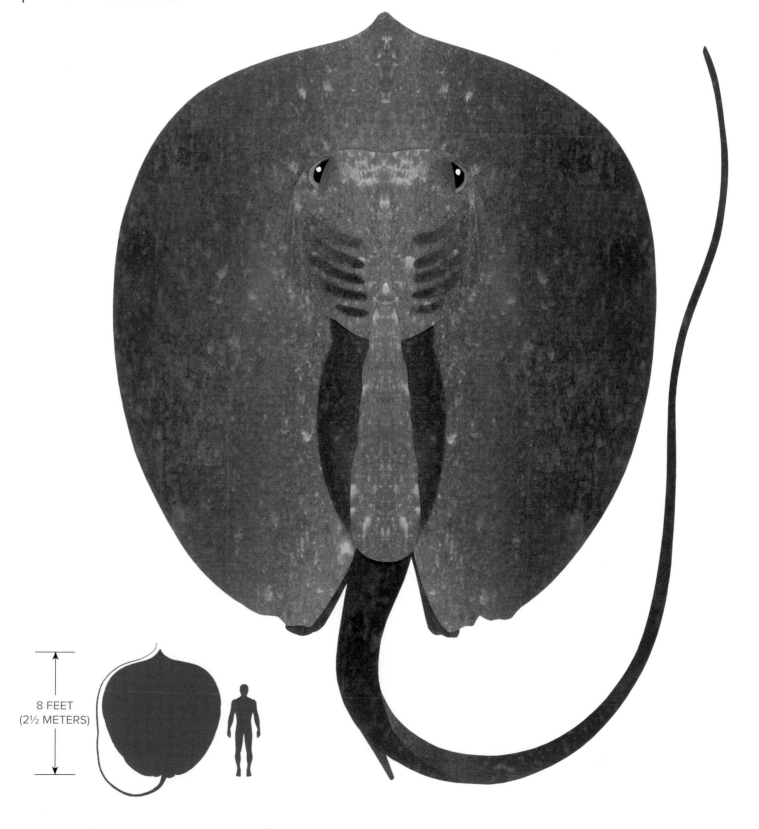

8 FEET
(2½ METERS)

Speedy bear

The extinct **giant short-faced bear** was a huge
North American predator. It could probably
run faster than any other animal its size, past or
present. With its long legs, it chased down horses
and deer and devoured them.

Few modern
carnivores could
compete with the
size, power, and killing
ability of many extinct
hunters—the apex
predators of the past.

The giant short-faced bear may have
been hunted to extinction by our
ancestors. It disappeared around the
time that the first humans arrived in the
Americas.

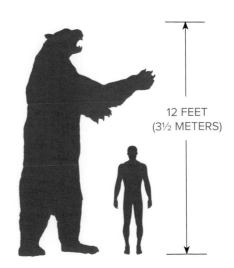

12 FEET
(3½ METERS)

Two-legged terror

The flightless **terror bird** was a fast runner that hunted small animals, probably killing them with blows of its huge beak. It may also have fed on the bodies of dead animals.

For millions of years, these birds were the dominant predators in South America. The largest of them weighed as much as a present-day lion or tiger.

10 FEET
(3 METERS)

Fangs—and a pouch

The **marsupial saber-tooth** lived in South America. It was probably an ambush hunter, leaping on a deer or other grazing animal and stabbing it to death with its curved canine teeth.

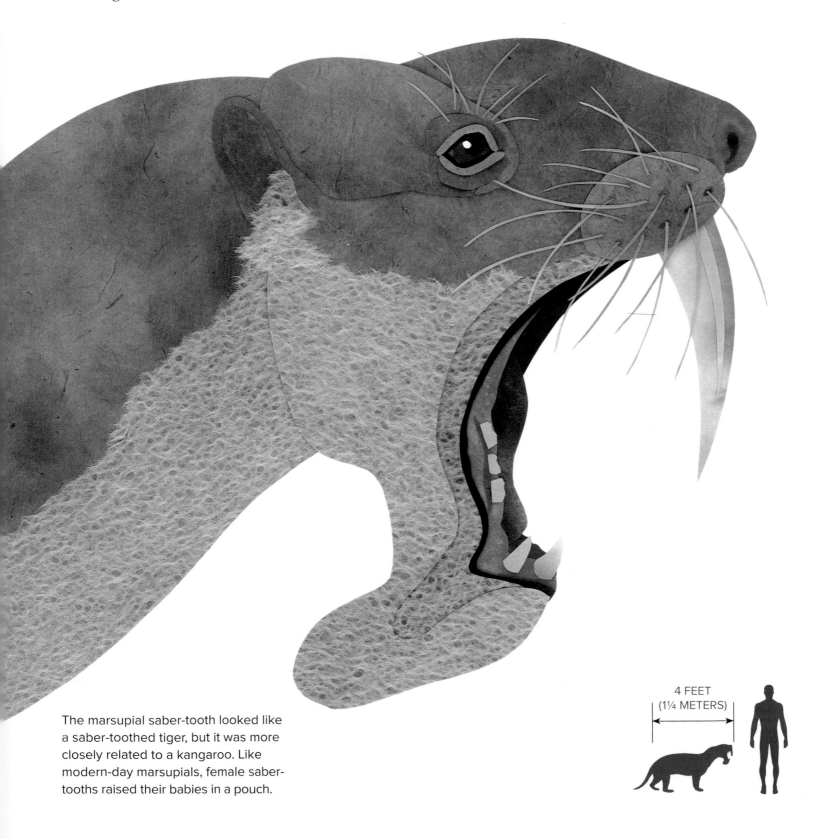

The marsupial saber-tooth looked like a saber-toothed tiger, but it was more closely related to a kangaroo. Like modern-day marsupials, female saber-tooths raised their babies in a pouch.

4 FEET
(1¼ METERS)

Big bird

The **giant** *Teratorn* (*tare-ah-torn*) was the largest bird to ever fly. It hunted small animals—mammals, reptiles, and other birds—by swooping down, grabbing them, and swallowing them whole.

23 FEET
(7 METERS)

This enormous bird lived in South America. It was too heavy to take flight simply by flapping its wings, so it probably launched itself into the air from a cliff or tree.

Killer pig

Daedon (*dy-don*) hunted large grazing animals, dispatching them with its tusks and powerful jaws. This North American mammal was an omnivore, occasionally feeding on plants or scavenging the kills of other predators.

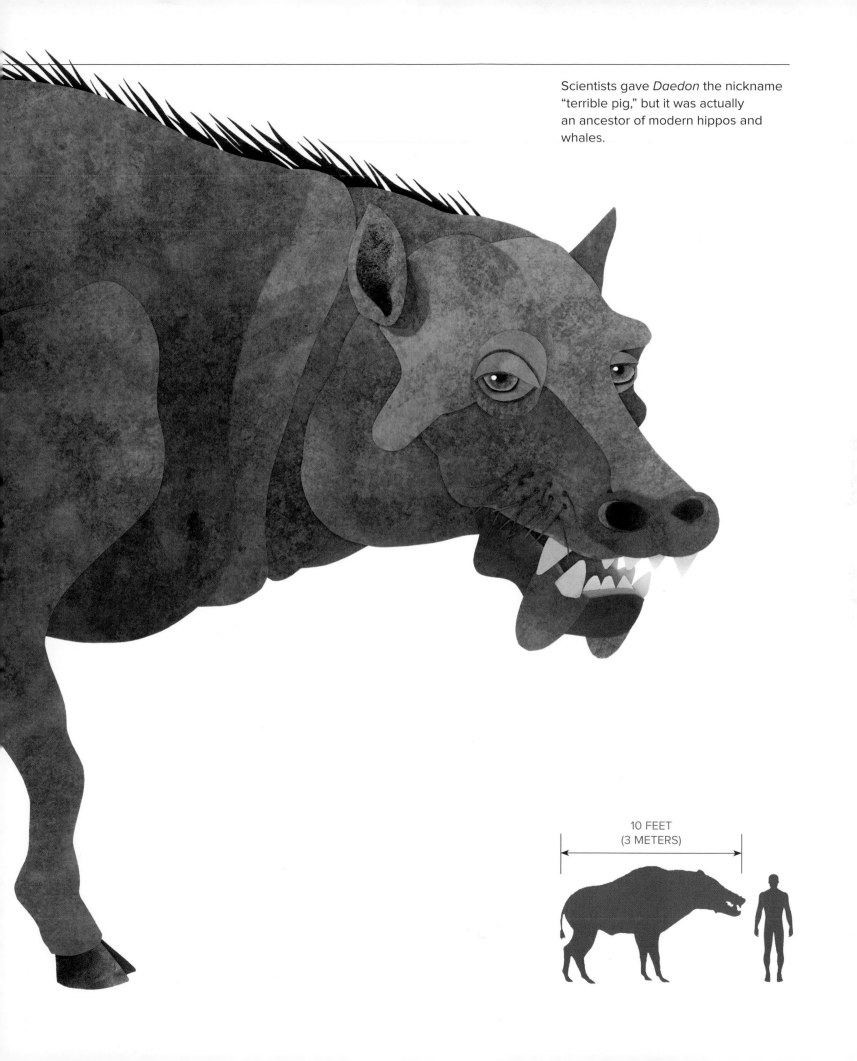

Scientists gave *Daedon* the nickname "terrible pig," but it was actually an ancestor of modern hippos and whales.

10 FEET
(3 METERS)

Monster snake

As far as we know, *Titanoboa* (*ty-tan-o-bo-ah*) was the largest snake that has ever lived. It spent much of its time in the water, where it preyed on crocodiles and fish.

Titanoboa lived in the tropical forests of what is now South America. It was longer than a school bus and weighed more than one ton (900 kilograms).

48 FEET
(14½ METERS)

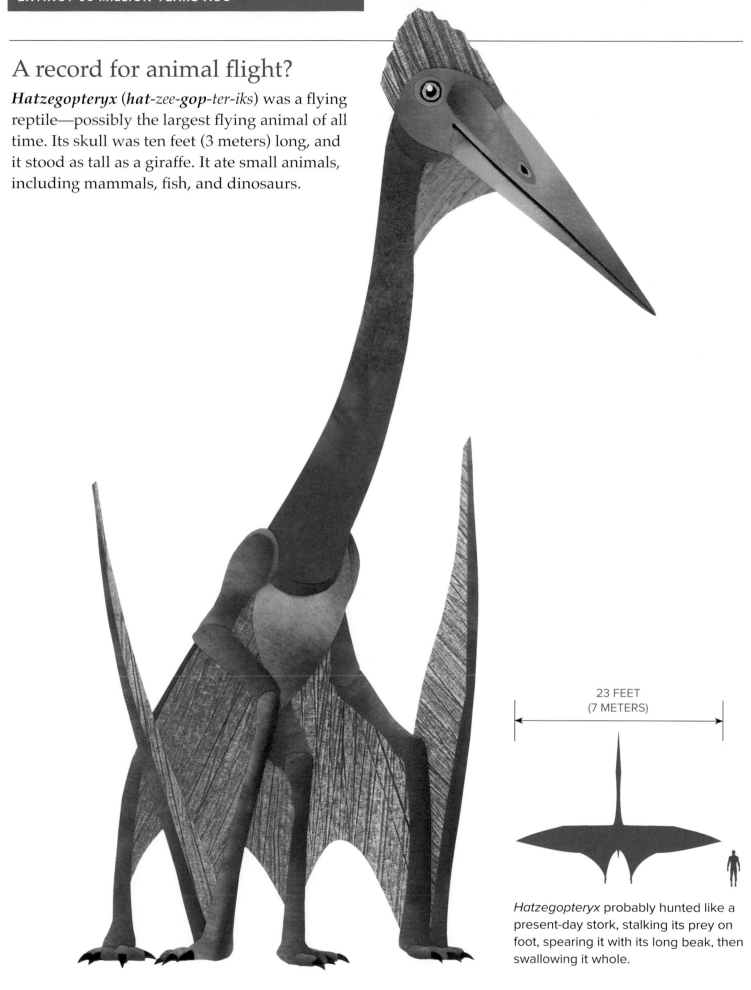

A record for animal flight?

Hatzegopteryx (**hat-zee-gop-ter-iks**) was a flying reptile—possibly the largest flying animal of all time. Its skull was ten feet (3 meters) long, and it stood as tall as a giraffe. It ate small animals, including mammals, fish, and dinosaurs.

23 FEET
(7 METERS)

Hatzegopteryx probably hunted like a present-day stork, stalking its prey on foot, spearing it with its long beak, then swallowing it whole.

Sea monster

During the age of the dinosaurs, the seas were ruled by the *Mosasaurs* (**moh**-*suh-sawrs*)— enormous predatory reptiles. One of the largest was **Tylosaurus** (*ty-lo-**sahr**-us*). Its formidable jaws were ten feet (3 meters) long, and it ate just about anything it wanted to, including other marine reptiles, fish, and dinosaurs that ventured into the water.

Mosasaurs such as *Tylosaurus* were the dominant predators in the oceans for 20 million years, but they died out with the dinosaurs 66 million years ago.

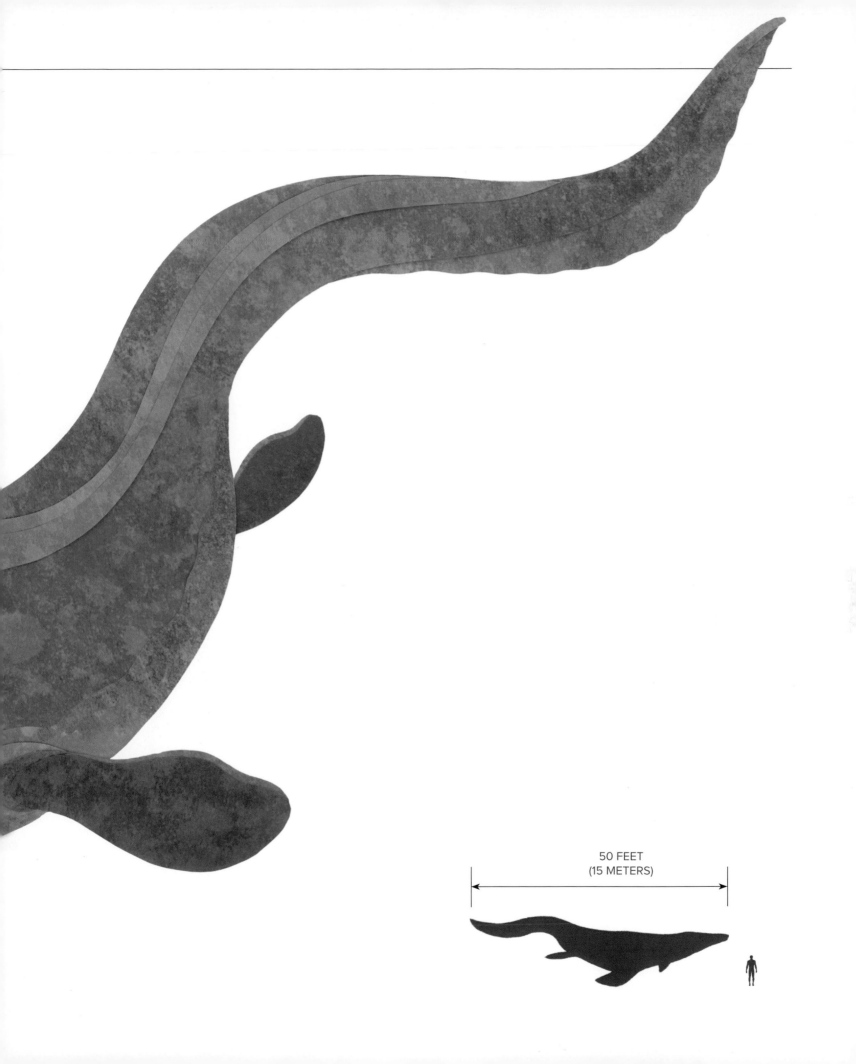

50 FEET
(15 METERS)

Swimming dinosaur

Tyrannosaurus rex may be more famous, but **Spinosaurus** (**spine**-*ah-sawr-us*) is the largest predatory dinosaur yet discovered. It was a good swimmer, and it hunted fish and other marine animals.

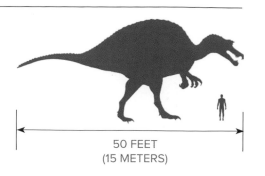

50 FEET
(15 METERS)

The sail on *Spinosaurus*'s back might have been used for signaling a mate or regulating its body temperature.

Deadly claw

Raptors were agile, intelligent predators. The smallest of these dinosaurs was the size of a chicken. **Utahraptor** (*yoo-taw-rap-ter*), one of the largest, reached twenty feet (6 meters) in length. Utahraptors may have hunted in packs, preying on plant-eating dinosaurs. A pack of these killers working together could have taken down dinosaurs much larger than themselves.

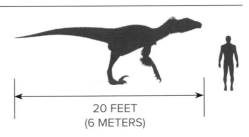

20 FEET
(6 METERS)

Utahraptor had big jaws and sharp teeth, but its main weapon was a curved "killing claw" more than 9 inches (23 centimeters) long.

Ancient amphibian

Mastodonsaurus (***mas***-*tuh*-*don*-***sawr***-*us*), an
ancient relative of today's salamanders, was a
predatory amphibian. It could walk on land, but
it probably spent much of its time in the water,
where it preyed on fish and smaller amphibians.

20 FEET
(6 METERS)

For millions of years before the
dinosaurs took over, huge amphibians
such as *Mastodonsaurus* were the
apex predators on land.

It *looked* like a dinosaur...

... and **Dimetrodon** (*dy-meet-ruh-don*) is often mistaken for one. But it lived 40 million years before the dinosaurs, and it was more closely related to mammals. It was a fearsome predator —probably the top carnivore of its time. It ate fish, amphibians, and other animals.

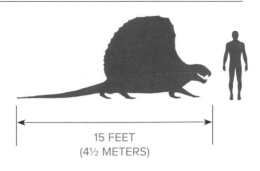

15 FEET
(4½ METERS)

Dimetrodon's big sail probably helped control its body temperature. It might also have been used to signal and attract a mate.

Armor-plated fish

Dunkleosteus (*dun-klee-**aw**-stee-us*) was an armor-plated fish that could have preyed on any sea creature of its time.

Three hundred and seventy-five million years ago, small animals had just begun to colonize the land. In the seas, however, predators had reached an impressive size. *Dunkleosteus* was one of the largest and fiercest of these carnivores.

33 FEET
(10 METERS)

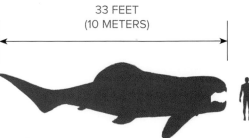

Sea-floor killer

The **sea scorpion** was among the largest animals alive 400 million years ago. It hunted smaller animals on the sea floor, and it may have been a scavenger as well.

Sea scorpions were some of the first arthropods, a group of animals that includes insects, spiders, scorpions, crabs, and lobsters.

8 FEET
(2½ METERS)

Out of the water

Plants were among the first living things to leave the sea and live on land. They were followed by mites and other tiny animals that fed on the plants. Once plant-eating animals had colonized the land, predators followed. One of these early hunters was **Trigonotarbid** (**trig**-*oh*-*no*-**tar**-*bid*), an animal similar to modern spiders.

1 INCH
(2½ CENTIMETERS)

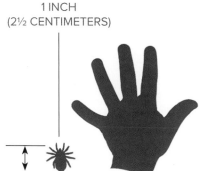

When *Trigonotarbid* arrived on the scene it didn't have much competition from other predators, so it didn't have to be large to be an apex predator.

Strange shrimp

When **Anomalocaris** (*ah-nom-moh-low-**ker**-is*) was alive, some 500 million years ago, animals lived only in the sea—none had made the move to land. *Anomalocaris* was perhaps the largest animal and the top predator of its time. It hunted and ate smaller ocean-dwelling creatures.

6½ FEET
(2 METERS)

Anomalocaris was named "strange shrimp" because scientists at first thought that fossils of the creature's mouth parts were individual shrimplike animals, not pieces of a larger animal.

This book describes a few creatures at the top of their food chains. Some are living today, while others are long gone. We will never see a fight between a modern apex predator and one that is extinct, but it's interesting to imagine what might happen if a predator from the present could face off with one from the distant past . . .

A matchup between a tiger and *Spinosaurus*, pictured here at the same scale, would not even be close. This dinosaur, the largest land predator of all time, could easily bite the big cat in half.

How would a **Siberian tiger** fare in a fight with ***Utahraptor,*** a top predator of 125 million years ago? The tiger is quick and powerful. Its claws and teeth are deadly weapons. But the dinosaur is also fast, and it weighs twice as much as the tiger. The big cat is probably smarter. And it might be able to outmaneuver the raptor, leap on its back, and bite its neck. But if the Utahraptor can get in a slash with one of its deadly killing claws, the fight will probably be over.

What about a battle between two ocean-dwelling carnivores? What would happen if a **great white shark** faced *Dunkleosteus,* an armored fish that ruled the seas 400 million years ago? A great white can be more than 20 feet (6 meters) long, with one of the most forceful bites of any living animal. *Dunkleosteus* is bigger, however, reaching 33 feet (10 meters) in length. It also has a powerful set of jaws.

The shark is much quicker than the heavily armored prehistoric fish. But that armor gives *Dunkleosteus* what could be an overwhelming advantage. The shark can dodge and attack more easily than its opponent. But its teeth, made to tear the soft flesh of seals and fish, will have a hard time biting through the armored skin of its opponent. One bite from the ancient fish's bony jaws could be fatal for the shark.

There isn't much point imagining a fight between *Tylosaurus* and a great white shark—this huge marine reptile could kill anything living in the ocean today.

The deadliest predator

There is one apex predator—the most deadly and efficient predator that has ever lived—that has not been described in this book. This predator, of course, is us. Humans do not have deadly fangs or claws. Compared to a tiger or shark, we are slow and weak. But we've made up for it with our big brains, our clever hands, and our ability to cooperate. We've invented weapons more powerful than those of any creature. And over the centuries we have killed off many of the large predators that threatened our lives or competed with us for food.

For Robin

Bibliography

Books:

Animal Fact File. By Tony Hare. Checkmark Books, 1999.

Atlas of the Prehistoric World. By Douglas Palmer. Discovery Books, 1999.

Dinosaur Encyclopedia. Edited by Kitty Blount and Maggie Crowley. DK Publishing, 2001.

Encyclopedia of Dinosaurs and Other Prehistoric Creatures. By John Malam and Steve Parker. Backpack Books, 2004.

Ice Age Mammals of North America. By Ian M. Lange. Mountain Press Publishings, 2002.

National Geographic Animal Encyclopedia. By Jinny Johnson. Marshall Editions, 1999.

Prehistoric Predators. By Brian Switek. Applesauce Press, 2015.

Reptiles. Edited by Dr. Allen E. Greer. Time Life Books, 1996.

Websites:

www.amnh.org (the American Museum of Natural History)

www.nationalgeographic.com

www.sciencedaily.com

www.sciencemag.org

www.scientificamerican.com

www.si.edu (the Smithsonian Institution)

To learn about the making of *Apex Predators,* visit **stevejenkinsbooks.com/predators.**

www.hmhco.com

The illustrations in this book are torn- and cut-paper collage.
The text type in this book is Palatino and Proxima Nova.
The display type in this book is Trixie.

Library of Congress Cataloging-in-Publication Data
Names: Jenkins, Steve, 1952– author.
Title: Apex predators : the world's deadliest hunters, past and present / Steve Jenkins.
Description: Boston ; New York : Houghton Mifflin Harcourt, [2017] | Audience: Ages 6–9. | Audience: K to grade 3.
Identifiers: LCCN 2016020040 | ISBN 9780544671607 (hardcover)
Subjects: LCSH: Predatory animals—Juvenile literature. | Predation (Biology)—Juvenile literature.
Classification: LCC QL758 .J46 2017 | DDC 591.5/3—dc23 LC record available at https://lccn.loc.gov/2016020040

Manufactured in China
SCP 10 9 8 7 6 5 4 3 2 1
4500646562